# Diana
## Princess of the People

*by*

TANYA LEE STONE

*A Gateway Biography   The Millbrook Press   Brookfield, Connecticut*

# Diana

## Princess of the People

**St. Louis de Montfort Catholic School**
**Fishers, IN**

Cover photographs courtesy of © Tim Graham/
Sygma; © Leo de Wys, Inc./D&J Heaton.

Photographs courtesy of © Dave Chancellor/Alpha/
Globe Photos, Inc.: pp. 3, 6; Alpha/Globe Photos, Inc.:
pp. 9, 14-15, 26; AP/Wide World Photos: pp. 12, 38,
40; Keystone/Sygma: p.19; © Tim Graham/Sygma: pp.
20, 25, 32, 35, 37; Sygma: pp. 22, 30

Stone, Tanya Lee.
Diana : princess of the people / Tanya Lee Stone.
p.   cm. — (Gateway biography)
Includes bibliographical references (p.    ) and index.
Summary: Follows the life of Diana, Princess of Wales,
from her childhood, through her experiences with the
royal family and public life, to her death in 1997.
ISBN 0-7613-1262-5 (lib. bdg.)
1. Diana, Princess of Wales, 1961–1997—Juvenile
literature. 2. Princesses—Great Britain—Biography—
Juvenile literature. [1. Diana, Princess of Wales, 1961–
1997. 2. Princesses. 3. Women—Biography.]
I. Title. II. Series.
DA591.A45D5255   1999
941.085'092—dc21
[B]   98-27988   CIP   AC

Published by The Millbrook Press, Inc.
2 Old New Milford Road
Brookfield, Connecticut 06804

For Princesses Stefanie, Elonna, Sarah,
and Prince Jacob

n August 31, 1997, millions of people heard the sorrowful news that Princess Diana of Wales had been killed in a car accident. The shock was felt around the world. Diana Spencer, the most admired and beloved member of the royal family, was only thirty-six years old. Even though she died at such a young age, Princess Diana had already made an enormous impact on the world.

Diana cared deeply for people. She spent much time doing charitable work to benefit children's hospitals, patients with AIDS, homeless people, cancer hospitals, leprosy patients, and the English National Ballet. In addition to devoting herself to these causes, Diana also supported about ninety other charities. Although she was royalty, Diana Spencer was truly the people's princess.

*Diana Frances Spencer* was born on July 1, 1961, in her family's home of Park House in Norfolk County, England. Her father, Edward John Spencer (Johnnie), held the title Viscount Althorp. Her mother was the Honorable Frances Burke Roche.

Diana had two older sisters, Sarah and Jane. Before Diana was born, her mother had given birth to a son. Tragically, he lived for only a few hours. Her parents had desperately wanted a son to carry on the family name. Frances became pregnant again, and they hoped the baby would be a boy. When Diana was born, her father was disappointed that she was not the son he had wished for. Although he always had a special place in his heart for Diana, she felt her father's disappointment. For the rest of her life, she carried with her feelings of guilt and failure. "I was the girl who was supposed to be a boy," she recalled.

Three years after Diana was born, the Spencers did have a son, Charles Edward. He was treated like royalty. His godmother was the Queen of England, and he was christened at Westminster Abbey.

*Diana's early childhood* had many happy times. Park House, on royal property in Norfolk County, was rented from the Queen. It was a big, beautiful house, and there were all kinds of animals for the children to play with. Diana was especially fond of animals. She had a cat named Marmalade, a springer spaniel named

Diana had a privileged childhood but always sensed her parents' disappointment that she hadn't been born a boy.

Jill, and a guinea pig named Peanuts. The family also had rabbits, hamsters, and horses. When she was three years old, Diana learned to ride a horse.

The children's favorite room at Park House was one they had decorated themselves. Called "The Beatle Room" after the rock group The Beatles, it had posters and pictures of many of the music stars of the 1960s. Diana also loved her bedroom, where she had a view of parkland and fields dotted with grazing cattle.

It was not uncommon in England for upper-class families to have a governess to take care of the children. The Spencers' governess taught the children at home until they were old enough to attend school. They also ate most of their meals with her.

Although the Spencers were a privileged family, the children were taught to treat all people with equal respect. They learned to accept people for who they were and not what social position they held. Diana and her brothers and sisters were also taught the importance of honesty and good manners. Partly because of this upbringing, Diana was always well-liked wherever she went.

When Diana was just six years old, in the summer of 1967, her parents separated. For the rest of her life, she would vividly remember the moment that her mother packed her bags and left to live in London. Diana sat at the bottom of the stairs and listened to the car door shut and the engine fade away into the distance. Making things worse for Diana, her sisters Sarah and Jane left for West Heath boarding school about the same time. A few weeks after her mother had gone to London, Diana and Charles went there to live with her. They visited their father on the weekends. This living arrangement continued until Christmas.

After the holiday, Diana's father insisted that the children return to Park House. He wanted them to attend the nearby Silfield school. Diana spent two years at Silfield and was an average student. But her teachers remember that she was talented in art class and went out of her way to be kind to other children.

In April 1969, Diana's parents were divorced. Her father, Johnnie, got custody of the children, meaning that legally they were to continue living with him. This was a difficult time for Diana. Although she disguised it well, she was sad, confused, and lonely. But she acted as normally as she could, playing with her animals, riding her tricycle, and helping her younger brother.

One month later, on May 2, Diana's mother was remarried, to a man named Peter Shand Kydd. Diana visited them on week-

Now Lady Diana at age fourteen, she poses with Soufflé,
a Shetland pony at her mother's home in Scotland.

ends and during school vacations. Her mother was happier than she had been in a long time, and this made Diana feel much better, too. The children liked Peter, and he loved to take them sailing.

When Diana was nine years old, she went away to a boarding school named Riddlesworth Hall. To her delight, she was able to take her guinea pig Peanuts with her. At Riddlesworth, Diana's self-confidence grew and her personality bloomed. She made a lot of friends and loved to help out with the younger children. In fact, she was honored with the Legatt Cup, an award for helpfulness.

After Riddlesworth, Diana spent four years at West Heath boarding school—the same one that her older sisters had attended. As at Riddlesworth, she was an average student, but she made important friendships that would last her whole life. She also studied dance, played tennis, and read countless romance novels by Barbara Cartland. Diana won many trophies for swimming and diving at West Heath and even invented a dive called the "Spencer Special," which always drew a crowd.

While she was at West Heath, Diana discovered that she had a passion and talent for working with needy people. Through a school volunteer program, she visited patients at Darenth Park, a hospital for the mentally ill. She found that this type of work helped her self-esteem and gave her a sense of accomplishment. Diana would grow up to have an enormous impact on the lives of the needy all over the world.

In June 1975, Diana's paternal grandfather, the seventh Earl Spencer, died. Johnnie then became the eighth Earl Spencer. And at the age of fourteen, Diana became Lady Diana. Her sisters also acquired the title of Lady before their names. Her brother Charles, at the age of eleven, became the new Viscount Althorp.

A few years earlier, in the fall of 1972, the seventh Earl Spencer's wife had died. Diana had adored her grandmother, Countess Spencer. The Countess often volunteered to visit the sick and always had a kind word for people. She had been an inspiration to Diana.

With the grandfather's estate now empty, the family moved from Park House to Althorp, which had been in the family for 450 years. It was located in Northamptonshire, about two hours from London. The children were unhappy about the move.

*The Spencers moved to Althorp, which had been Diana's grandfather's home. The children didn't care for the darkness and formality of this estate that had been in their family for 450 years.*

Unlike Park House, Althorp was formal, dark, and stuffy, and they missed their friends. Diana's memories of visiting Althorp when she was younger were bleak. Althorp had dark corridors and portraits of long-dead ancestors that gave her and Charles the shivers. After a while they adjusted to their new home. The one thing that Diana did love about Althorp was that it had beautiful places for her to dance. She would often practice ballet when she thought no one was watching.

On July 14, 1976, Diana's father married a woman named Raine, who was the Countess of Dartmouth. Barbara Cartland, the romance novelist Diana so loved, was Raine's mother. But this did not help the situation. The children did not like Raine at all. Before the two were married, Charles sent Raine a note telling her just how he felt, and Diana had a friend send Raine a nasty letter. And whenever the sisters were together and Raine's name would come up, they would all sing, "Raine, Raine, go away, come again some other day!"

When Diana was a young girl growing up in Park House, the vacation house of England's royal family was walking distance away. Diana and her family saw them occasionally while the royal family was on vacation. Diana's sister Sarah began dating Prince Charles, the oldest son. In November 1977, Sarah invited Diana to come home from boarding school for a weekend party, at which

Prince Charles would be a guest. Although Diana, who was just sixteen, developed a secret crush on the prince, Charles, who was twenty-nine, did not take a special interest in her.

Just after her eighteenth birthday, in 1979, Diana moved into her own apartment in London. She lived with three room-mates—Carolyn Pride, Anne Bolton, and Virginia Pitman. Diana got a job teaching three days a week at the Young England kindergarten. As always, she was wonderful with the children, and she loved her job. The other two days she was a governess for an American family living in London. She also began to have more contact with the royal family because her sister Jane was married to the Queen's assistant secretary, Robert Fellowes.

Diana had been invited to several events with the royal family. During one party, in July 1980, she sat next to Prince Charles. His grandfather had recently died. She told him, "You looked so sad . . . at the funeral. . . . You are lonely, you should be with somebody to look after you." After that, Charles took an interest in Diana, and they began dating. By the fall, news of their romance had spread.

At the same time, people knew that Prince Charles was more interested in finding a woman that would fill the role of princess than he was in falling in love. He once said, "Marriage is a much more important business than falling in love.

. . . I have a particular responsibility to ensure that I make the right decision."

Charles Philip Arthur George was the eldest son of Queen Elizabeth II and Prince Philip. He was named Prince of Wales when he was just ten years old. This is the title that is given to the first male heir to the British throne. Charles knew that it was his responsibility to present an image of being suitable as a future king. He served in the royal navy and represented the Queen all over the world. The British people were always curious to know everything about him, including whom he was dating. After he turned thirty, he began to feel pressured to get married. He liked Diana because she was fun, honest, and always herself. She was also in love with him.

Although Prince Charles was used to constant attention from the media, Diana wasn't. Once word got out that she was dating Charles, reporters would wait for her to come out of her apartment and photograph her. Sometimes she would wear a disguise and sneak out. Nevertheless, both the public and the royal family were impressed by the friendly way she handled the situation.

On February 24, 1981, the engagement of Prince Charles and Lady Diana was announced. The British people were thrilled with Charles's choice. It seemed like a fairy-tale romance. Diana

# Earls, Dukes, and Princes

You may have noticed that many British people you hear about in the news have titles in front of their names. This can be confusing. In Britain, both the royal family and members of the aristocracy (upper class, or nobility) have titles.

Diana's family was part of the British aristocracy. This means that the family had a high social rank and that titles were passed along by birth. Diana's paternal grandfather (her father's father) was the seventh Earl Spencer. When he died, Diana's father became the eighth Earl Spencer. In turn, when Diana's father died, her brother Charles Edward became the ninth Earl Spencer.

In addition to the men in a family, the women are also given titles. The daughter of a duke, marquess, or earl has the title of Lady before her name. So, when Diana's father became Earl Spencer, she became Lady Diana.

These titles can get even more complicated! When a woman marries a man whose title outranks that of her father, she then takes her husband's title. That is why when Lady Diana married the Prince of Wales she became known as the Princess of Wales.

*Unlike Diana, Prince Charles had spent his entire life in the public eye and was used to the attention. He is pictured here at about age nineteen, on the day of his official designation as Prince of Wales. His mother, the Queen, walks with him.*

Millions around the world followed the courtship of
Charles and Diana. People were enchanted by the idea of
the charming Diana capturing the heart of the prince.

now had to learn how to live as a princess. She moved out of her apartment into a suite of rooms at Buckingham Palace. Although she was excited about her new status in the royal family, she also felt lonely and anxious. Diana was in love with Prince Charles, but he often had a certain distance and formality toward her that was troubling. She soon became depressed, lost a lot of weight, and felt tired much of the time. She was discovering that becoming a princess was not like it was in fairy tales. She knew, though, that she loved Charles and that she would go ahead with the marriage.

*Charles and Diana* were married on July 29, 1981, at St. Paul's Cathedral in London. More than 2,500 guests attended the wedding. About 2 million people lined the streets leading to the cathedral in order to catch a glimpse of Diana's arrival. The wedding also was aired on television, attracting more than 750 million viewers. Diana arrived at the cathedral in a glass coach, and her father walked her down the aisle. The moment they were married, Diana officially became Her Royal Highness the Princess of Wales. It was also the last time that she would experience the freedom and privacy of being an ordinary citizen.

As the new royal couple made their way back to the Palace, the crowds that lined the streets of London cheered and waved. Diana's innocent and friendly nature was a breath of fresh air for the image of the royal family. The British people loved her and felt proud. The couple received more than 10,000 wedding presents. Approximately 1,000 of their wedding gifts were exhibited for eight weeks at St. James's Palace in London. More than 200,000 people paid an entrance fee to see the gifts and purchased souvenirs. The profits from this exhibit were donated to charity.

Diana had a difficult time adjusting to life as royalty. She was not used to formality and was unhappy much of the time. She developed an eating disorder called bulimia nervosa. Stress and depression often trigger this disorder. Lady Colin Campbell, who wrote a biography of Princess Diana, believes the problem began shortly after the wedding. "She saw engagement pictures of herself looking heavy, and she promptly went on a diet," says Campbell. "She ate practically nothing, but she [eventually] went on [eating] binges. Then she'd make herself sick." Another biographer, Andrew Morton, reported that Diana made shallow cuts on herself in a suicide gesture meant as a cry for help.

Charles couldn't understand why Diana was so miserable because he had grown up accustomed to strict rules and little

*The royal couple's wedding took place on July 29, 1981, and was aired on television.*

privacy. But a wonderful event in their lives eased the strain. On June 21, 1982, Diana gave birth to a son. They named him William Arthur Philip Louis, known as Prince William.

For a while, things seemed better. Charles and Diana were enjoying parenthood. They both thought that children should be brought up as normally as possible, and Diana spent all her free time with Prince William. Two years later, on September 15, 1984, the royal couple had another son, Prince Harry. Diana spent her time taking care of her children and attending endless events as a representative of the royal family. She enjoyed some of the functions she went to, but found others boring. As a twenty-four-year-old woman, she missed being able to relax and have fun with people her own age.

But then Princess Diana began to blossom from a shy, young girl into a more confident woman. Many people think that Sarah Ferguson, the Duchess of York, was partly responsible for this change in Diana. Sarah was married to Charles's brother, Prince Andrew. She was two years older than Diana, outgoing, confident, and fun. Sarah reminded Diana that they were young, and, though they had responsibilities as members of the royal family, there was nothing wrong with enjoying themselves.

Princess Diana began to associate with Sarah and a new group of young friends. Her improved self-esteem also helped

Diana and Charles seemed to be happiest as parents.
Prince William (held by Diana) was born June 21, 1982,
and Prince Harry was born September 15, 1984.

*Sarah Ferguson, the Duchess of York, who was known as Fergie, was a good friend to Diana and helped her to become more confident with her role in the royal family, and to have more fun, as well.*

her to adjust more comfortably to her role in the royal family. She was more at ease talking to people, and she quickly became one of the most popular women in the world. Other women wanted to dress like her, adopt her hairstyle, and copy anything about her that they could. She was constantly photographed and was affectionately known as Princess Di (although she never liked it). But while Diana felt happier, the royal couple's marriage became strained.

Charles did not approve of Diana's going to parties with her new friends. And Diana objected to the amount of time that he had to spend traveling and attending official events, all of which took him away from his family. They liked different things and began to spend more time apart than together. In 1986 her bulimia got worse. She spoke out about her experience, saying that victims of eating disorders do not harm their bodies merely to lose weight. Usually they do so because they feel bad about themselves as people and want to hurt themselves.

In December 1992, the prince and princess officially separated. Diana, however, had begun to see that she could accomplish important things as part of the royal family. She had always had a special place in her heart for children and the needy. By 1988, in addition to her official duties, the Princess of Wales was involved with twenty-nine different charities. By 1996 that number had grown to one hundred.

That same year, on August 28, Diana and Charles were divorced. Although she lost the title Her Royal Highness, Diana was still officially recognized as a member of the royal family. And her popularity was such that the general public and the media still referred to her as Princess Diana. It was close to the time of her divorce that Diana decided to focus her charitable work on six main categories: AIDS, homelessness, cancer, leprosy, children, and the English National Ballet. However, it didn't take long for this list to expand. She had a tendency to get involved with any cause she felt was worthwhile. Princess Diana took her charitable work seriously. On an average day, it was not unusual for her to visit three or four organizations. She talked to patients, attended benefits, did fund-raising, and completed a variety of other tasks for the charities she was committed to.

Princess Diana worked to help victims of AIDS (acquired immunodeficiency syndrome). This is an illness that may develop when a person contracts HIV (human immunodeficiency virus). AIDS affects a person's immune system, and millions of people have died from this terrible illness. Many people were prejudiced toward AIDS patients for fear that exposure to them might spread the disease to themselves.

Princess Diana was one of the first public figures to teach people that it is safe to touch people with AIDS. She said, "HIV does not make people dangerous to know, so you can shake their hands and give them a hug. Heaven knows, they need it." Diana attended the openings of AIDS wards in hospitals, visited AIDS patients all over the world, and gave benefits in support of organizations such as Britain's National AIDS Trust, CRUSAID, and The Elton John AIDS Foundation.

As with AIDS patients, fear and superstition surround people who have leprosy. Because leprosy has symptoms that can be unpleasant to look at, lepers have long been separated from society. People also thought that the disease was contagious and that they would contract it through contact with lepers. Princess Diana wanted to reach out to these patients and help get rid of the misconceptions about the disease.

In 1989 she traveled to Indonesia and visited patients at the Sitanala Leprosy Hospital. And in 1990 she went to a leper hospital in Nigeria. During both visits, Diana shook the hands of hundreds of patients, making sure that the television crews showed the world. She also sat on their beds, listening and talking with them. A doctor at the Nigerian hospital, Kate Dawson, said, "The Princess has helped so much. She has shown by being so open and natural with them that lepers are not a threat to anybody."

The media attention that Diana drew could often be used in positive ways, such as illustrating the humanitarian work she was accomplishing. But the constant flash of photography followed her everywhere she went. Diana hated being hounded by the press and often yearned to be left in peace. Sometimes

Diana talks with leprosy patients in Nepal in 1988. She seemed most drawn to those who were rejected by society. She once commented that "the biggest disease this world suffers from is the disease of people feeling unloved."

she was able to dodge the photographers. Diana contributed to many organizations dedicated to helping homeless people. One London shelter volunteer remembers that Diana often quietly slipped in to talk to the people there—even without the attention of the media. She also brought her sons with her, passing on her legacy of kindness to humanity.

In fact, her children remained her top priority. She was a dedicated mother and close to both of her sons. "In June 1992," recalls Mary Robertson, for whom Diana had been a governess, "we were traveling through England, and we had lunch at Kensington Palace with Diana and Prince Harry. She had just been to see William playing in a soccer game, so she was a little bit late in coming to see us, but she was exuberant, greeted us with a big hug. . . . It was very clear as we talked over lunch that her boys were the most important thing for her. She said to us, 'They are my life.'"

Princess Diana was also active in charities that focused on the needs of children. One of the many organizations she worked for was Birthright, which raises funds for research on problems in unborn children. One of the founders of Birthright said of Diana, "We could never have done what we did without the Princess of Wales. [Birthright] was a relatively new charity, and she helped to put us on the map."

Despite the pressures of the royal family and public life and the
unraveling of her marriage, Diana remained most devoted to her sons,
William and Harry. They are pictured here at Niagara Falls in 1991.

Diana was a supporter of the Great Ormond Street Hospital for Children in London, and she regularly went there to visit with the patients. She spent time with children at other hospitals as well. Many of the children had serious diseases, including cerebral palsy, and she liked to cheer them up and make them laugh. In 1995, United Cerebral Palsy honored Diana with an award for her work with children. Henry Kissinger, former U.S. secretary of state, presented her with the Humanitarian Award on December 12 in New York City.

In addition, Diana worked to help the elderly, whose needs had often gone unnoticed in Britain. With Diana's help, fund-raisers for an organization called Help the Aged became some of the most fashionable events of the year.

Princess Diana was also committed to getting laws passed that would ban the use of land mines worldwide. Land mines are explosive weapons that are buried in the ground. There are about 110 million land mines in 64 countries around the world. These mines were buried during times of war and can explode at any time. They kill and maim approximately 20,000 innocent people each year. In her quest to ban land mines, Princess Diana traveled to foreign countries, including Angola and Bosnia, to comfort victims and inspect dangerous areas.

In June 1997, Diana passionately addressed a crowd at an American Red Cross fund-raiser for the victims of land mines.

"These mines inflict most of their casualties on people who are trying to meet the elementary needs of life," she said. "They strike the women gathering firewood for cooking. They ambush the child sent to collect water for the family." Her work led to a heightened international awareness of the problem, as well as to the British government's announcement to ban land mines.

The work that Princess Diana was accomplishing was extraordinary. She was making the most out of her position as royalty and touching the lives of millions with her generosity and kindness. The news of her death on August 31, 1997, was hard to bear for many people around the world. At the time of the accident, Diana was in Paris with her friend Emad Mohamed al-Fayed, who was known as Dodi Fayed. The two were traveling in a limousine. A car crash took both of their lives.

The royal family's initial response to Diana's death was not emotional enough to suit the public who loved her. People were grieving, and many were angered by the royal family's brief announcement about her death, the lack of flags flying at half-mast, and the short funeral procession that was planned. The royal family quickly responded to the people's wishes and made

*One of the causes Diana devoted the most time to toward the end of her life was the banning of land mines. She is pictured here in Angola in 1997 with a young land-mine victim.*

plans to accommodate the crowds that wanted to mourn for Diana. Prince Charles, William, and Harry were in Scotland when Diana died, and, before returning to London, Charles spent some time with his sons in private. When they did arrive at Kensington Palace, the three of them greeted people, accepting flowers and sympathy wishes from some of the mourners outside the palace. The Queen also gave a heartfelt statement.

A *funeral* was held for Diana, Princess of Wales, on September 6, 1997, at Westminster Abbey. Millions of people crowded into London from all over Britain and elsewhere in the world to pay their respects. More than one million bouquets of flowers, which could be seen from airplanes flying overhead, were stacked outside the royal palaces. Speaking at her funeral, Diana's brother said, "Diana was the very essence of compassion, of duty, of style, of beauty. All over the world she was a symbol of selfless humanity." In the United States, more than 30 million people awoke in the middle of the night to watch the televised funeral.

After Diana's death, a foundation was set up to raise money for her favorite charities. It is called the Diana, Princess of Wales

From left to right are Diana's brother, Charles Earl Spencer, her sons, Prince William and Prince Harry, and her former husband, Prince Charles. Many people were critical of the royal family's reaction to Diana's death. It wasn't heartfelt enough, they thought.

Memorial Fund. Envelopes quickly flooded into the newly formed charity with donations ranging from coins that children had taped to handmade cards to large checks from corporations. Just six months after Diana's death, there was more than $66 million dollars in the fund. About half of that money was made from the sales of the Elton John song "Candle in the Wind 1997," which he sang at Princess Diana's funeral. Some of the organizations that benefited from this money were Centrepoint, a homeless charity; the English National Ballet; the Great Ormond Street Hospital Children's Charity; the National AIDS Trust; and the Leprosy Mission.

During her lifetime, Princess Diana had dedicated herself to helping others. Prime Minister Tony Blair of Great Britain called her "the people's princess" as she had found a way to break through the traditional barriers of royalty that had long set them apart from the British people. She was adored while she was alive, and, as Tony Blair said, "she will remain in our hearts and our memories forever."

*Diana's coffin is carried out of Westminster Abbey at the conclusion of her funeral on September 6, 1997.*

# Important Dates

| | | |
|---|---|---|
| *1961* | July 1 | Diana Frances Spencer is born. |
| *1969* | April | Parents Johnnie and Frances are divorced. |
| | May | Diana's mother remarries, to Peter Shand Kydd. |
| *1975* | June | The seventh Earl Spencer dies. Diana becomes Lady Diana. |
| *1976* | July 14 | Diana's father marries Raine, Countess of Dartmouth. |
| *1977* | November | Diana meets Prince Charles for the first time. |
| *1979* | | Diana gets a job teaching at the Young England kindergarten. |
| *1981* | February 24 | Princes Charles and Lady Diana announce their engagement. |
| | July 29 | Charles and Diana are married at St. Paul's Cathedral in London. |

| *1982* | June 21 | Prince William is born. |
| *1984* | September 15 | Prince Harry is born. |
| *1992* | December | The prince and princess separate. They are divorced in August 1996. |
| *1997* | August 31<br>September 6 | Princess Diana dies in an automobile accident.<br>The funeral for Diana is held. |

# *Organizations to Contact*

American Cancer Society
1599 Clifton Road NE
Atlanta, GA 30329

American Red Cross (to ban land mines)
8111 Gatehouse Road
Falls Church, VA 22042

Diana, Princess of Wales Memorial Fund
Kensington Palace
London W8 4PU
England

The Elton John AIDS Foundation
P.O. Box 2066
San Francisco, CA 94126-2066
(310) 535-1775
*ejaf@ejaf.org*

English National Ballet
Markova House
39 Jay Mews
London SW7 2BS
England

Leprosy Mission
80 Windmill Road
Brentford, Middlesex TW8 0QH
England
*www.leprosymission.org*

National Coalition for
   the Homeless
1012 Fourteenth Street NW, #600
Washington, DC 20005-3410
(202) 737-6444
*nch@uri.net*

The Pediatric AIDS Foundation
1311 Colorado Avenue
Santa Monica, CA 90404

# Sources Used

Apple, R.W., Jr. *Through London's Streets, the Sounds of Silence Toll.* New York Times, September 7, 1997.

*Brother's Eulogy for Diana*: "The Very Essence of Compassion." New York Times, September 7, 1997.

Campbell, Lady Colin. *Diana in Private: The Princess Nobody Knows.* New York: St. Martin's Press, 1992.

Carter, Bill. *Millions of Mourners.* New York Times, September 10, 1997.

Carter, Reon. *Booming Market in Di Memorabilia.* The Burlington Free Press, March 25, 1998.

Davies, Nicholas. *Diana: A Princess and Her Troubled Marriage.* New York: Birch Lane Press, 1992.

*Diana's Home Opens to the Public in July.* New York Times, December 14, 1997.

Hoge, Warren. *After a Funeral Befitting a Princess, Diana Will be Buried at Her Family Home.* New York Times, September 2, 1997.

Ibrahim, Youssef M. *Millions of Dollars Pouring in to Diana's Favorite Charities*. New York Times, September 9, 1997.

*In First Public Appearance, Charles Thanks Nation*. New York Times, September 20, 1997.

Licata, Renora. *Princess Diana: Royal Ambassador*. Woodbridge, CT: Blackbirch Press, 1993.

Morton, Andrew. *Diana: Her True Story*. New York: Simon & Schuster, 1992.

*100 Children Helped by Diana Visit Crash Site*. New York Times, September 22, 1997.

# *Index*

# About the Author

Tanya Lee Stone is a former editor of children's books who now writes full-time. She is the author of several books, including *Medical Causes*, from the Celebrity Activists series published by Twenty-First Century Books.

In addition to her writing, Tanya runs Project Angel Food, an organization that she founded in 1997. Project Angel Food gathers perishable foods that will be thrown out by supermarkets and restaurants and delivers them to shelters and community centers.

She lives in Burlington, Vermont, with her husband Alan and her son Jacob.